GW00724556

THE MOST EXCELLENT WAY

A Call to Walk in God's Love

BABATUNDE AKINFISOYE

KEBABI
PUBLICATIONS

THE MOST EXCELLENT WAY

Babatunde Akinfisoye

Published by Kebabi Publications

Text copyright © Babatunde Akinfisoye, 2017

First published 2018

ISBN 978-0-9926190-3-9

Edited by Andrew Halloway

Cover Design: Imaginovation Ltd.

Printed in UK by Kebabi Publications.

CONTENTS

ACKNOWLEDGEMENT

To the Almighty God who inspired me to write this book and led me in the direction of His Most Excellent Way.

PREFACE

A few years back, I felt the prompting to write this book, 'The Most Excellent Way'. My first three books had come in quick succession one after the other, but as soon as I started to write this one, I found out that I just could not continue.

I had to do a lot of soul searching, and I queried myself over and over again as to why I couldn't find a release in my spirit to continue. I concluded that I was not qualified to write a book about God's love (at least not at the time), as I needed to sort myself out and ensure that I had mastered (or at least have started) walking in 'The Most Excellent Way'.

It has been a few years since I received that prompting to write this book and I have just received the go-ahead in my spirit to recommence my work on it. While I cannot claim to be perfect or to have a complete understanding of love which Paul the apostle described as "the most excellent way" (1 Corinthians 12:31, NIV), I know I have grown through the years and at least have a better understanding of how to walk in this way.

Chapter 1

WHERE THE JOURNEY BEGINS

Being born again or becoming a Christian is the best thing that can ever happen to any human being. It is a passage from death to life and marks the beginning of a journey to 'Heaven' (our final place of rest with God).

Amazingly, becoming a Christian requires following a simple process of acknowledging the fact that we are sinners, and that we are unable to please God through our own human effort.

For everyone has sinned; we all fall short of God's glorious standard. Romans 3:23

Obviously our sins have grave consequences, but God in His lovingkindness graciously paid the price through the sacrifice of His Son. All who accept God's wonderful sacrifice escape the punishment of spiritual death as, through the Son, they gain a passage from death to life.

Acknowledging that we are sinners should therefore be followed by an acceptance of God's gracious sacrifice, by embracing His love and yielding one's self to Him.

> For the wages of sin is death, but the free gift of God is eternal life through Christ Jesus our Lord. Romans 6:23

Anyone who sincerely acknowledges that they are a sinner, and repents of their sins by turning to God and accepting the gracious sacrifice of His Son, becomes 'born again'. This is, however, the beginning of a whole new journey (a journey to God's kingdom, a journey to Heaven) and a whole new life, hence the term 'born again'.

> This means that anyone who belongs to Christ has become a new person. The old life is gone; a new life has begun! 2 Corinthians 5:17

Chapter 2

EQUIPPED TO SUCCEED

God never initiates anything without properly planning for it. In the same way, God never sends anyone on a journey or an assignment without properly equipping the person to succeed.

Before God created human beings in the book of Genesis in the Bible, God had created everything that they needed to survive and succeed. He created human beings last and gave them a purpose, having equipped them to succeed:

> Then God said, "Let the earth produce every sort of animal, each producing offspring of the same kind—livestock, small animals that scurry along the ground, and wild animals." And that is what happened. God made all sorts of wild animals, livestock, and small animals, each able to produce offspring of the same kind. And God saw that it was good.

3

Then God said, "Let us make human beings in our image, to be like us. They will reign over the fish in the sea, the birds in the sky, the livestock, all the wild animals on the earth, and the small animals that scurry along the ground."

So God created human beings in his own image. In the image of God he created them; male and female he created them.

Then God blessed them and said, "Be fruitful and multiply. Fill the earth and govern it. Reign over the fish in the sea, the birds in the sky, and all the animals that scurry along the ground."

Then God said, "Look! I have given you every seed-bearing plant throughout the earth and all the fruit trees for your food. And I have given every green plant as food for all the wild animals, the birds in the sky, and the small animals that scurry along the ground— everything that has life." And that is what happened.
Genesis 1:24–30

In the same way God plans and equips human beings for their

4

physical wellbeing, He also plans and equips us for our spiritual wellbeing.

When we yield our lives to Him, effectively becoming Christians, He comes to indwell our lives in the person of the Holy Spirit and through the Holy Spirit He equips us with all that we need to live successfully as Christians.

The Holy Spirit does two major things for us that we will explore in this book: -

1. He endows us with spiritual gifts that enhance our capabilities as children of God
2. He enables us to cultivate an excellent character.

If we correctly utilise the endowment of the Holy Spirit and follow His path for our lives, we will realise that we have been fully equipped to succeed.

Chapter 3

Our Life's Journey

Seeing that the main area of our focus is 'The Most Excellent Way', it might be a good idea for us to view our life's journey in terms of 'ways'. So, for the purpose of our understanding, I will be dividing our life's journey into three specific ways, two of which we will discuss in this chapter.

1. Our own self-led way
2. Our gifted way
3. The most excellent way

Our own self-led way

Every human being on earth, irrespective of whether they are Christians or not, individually decide on the path they want to tread – some choose 'good' and some choose 'bad'.

All of us, like sheep, have strayed away. We have left God's paths to follow our own. Yet the LORD laid on him the sins of us all. Isaiah 53:6

However, whether good or bad, each of these self-led ways actually leads us along the same path and toward the same destination away from God. It is only when we come in contact with God through our Lord and Saviour Jesus Christ, and so begin a new journey, that we move in the right direction.

If you investigate the lives of most human beings treading the self-led way, you will discover that as far as they are concerned, they are travelling in the right direction. They are totally oblivious to the fact that they are actually heading the wrong way.

There is a path before each person that seems right, but it ends in death. Proverbs 14:12

A self-led way equates to a life without God, and however humanly successful this kind of life may seem, it ends with an eternity of suffering and rejection apart from God.

It is therefore a great privilege when one is presented with an opportunity to accept Christ's sacrifice for our sins, invite Him into our lives and be led by His Spirit.

Our gifted way

While this second way is available to everyone, it is not automatic and can only be trod by those who accept God's sacrifice of His Son and therefore begin a new journey of life as God's adopted children.

> *He came into the very world he created, but the world didn't recognize him. He came to his own people, and even they rejected him. But to all who believed him and accepted him, he gave the right to become children of God. They are reborn—not with a physical birth resulting from human passion or plan, but a birth that comes from God. John 1:10–13*

In order to assist anyone who follows this new way and ensure their success, God deposits His Holy Spirit into their lives as a guarantee of His great promises for them.

> *It is God who enables us, along with you, to stand firm for*

9

Christ. He has commissioned us, and he has identified us as his own by placing the Holy Spirit in our hearts as the first instalment that guarantees everything he has promised us.
2 Corinthians 1:21–22

One of the things that the Holy Spirit does for us is that He endows us with spiritual gifts that enhance our capabilities as children of God, enabling us to travel along the gifted way.

The twelfth chapter of 1 Corinthians deals extensively with how the Holy Spirit endows us with various gifts and the purpose of such endowments. It is essential for everyone travelling along the path to God's kingdom to gain a full understanding of the gifts and the purposes for which the Holy Spirit has given them.

Now, dear brothers and sisters, regarding your question about the special abilities the Spirit gives us. I don't want you to misunderstand this. 1 Corinthians 12:1

With Paul's statement above in mind, we will endeavour in the remaining part of this chapter to clarify any misunderstanding about spiritual gifts or 'our gifted way'.

The first thing we need to note here is that the Holy Spirit is the source of every spiritual gift. And because the Holy Spirit is God, He works in consonance with the Trinity (God the Father, God the Son and God the Holy Spirit). This is why Paul the apostle stated in 1 Corinthians 12:3 that he wanted the Corinthian Christians to know "… that no one speaking by the Spirit of God will curse Jesus, and no one can say Jesus is Lord, except by the Holy Spirit." Paul further stated in the following verses that…

> There are different kinds of spiritual gifts, but the same Spirit is the source of them all. There are different kinds of service, but we serve the same Lord. God works in different ways, but it is the same God who does the work in all of us.
> 1 Corinthians 12:4–6

If anyone therefore claims to be operating a gift of the Spirit but curses Jesus, berates Him or does not operate in agreement with His Word, that person's claim is untrue and is certainly not operating a gift of the Holy Spirit.

The next thing to note is that **the Holy Spirit gives us spiritual gifts so that we can use them to assist each other along the path of our Christian journey.** The Holy Spirit predetermines what gift

He wants to give each individual Christian with the intent that we will collaborate and use our various giftings for the good of all.

A spiritual gift is given to each of us so we can help each other. To one person the Spirit gives the ability to give wise advice; to another the same Spirit gives a message of special knowledge. The same Spirit gives great faith to another, and to someone else the one Spirit gives the gift of healing. He gives one person the power to perform miracles, and another the ability to prophesy. He gives someone else the ability to discern whether a message is from the Spirit of God or from another spirit. Still another person is given the ability to speak in unknown languages, while another is given the ability to interpret what is being said. It is the one and only Spirit who distributes all these gifts. He alone decides which gift each person should have.
1 Corinthians 12:7–11

Sadly, a lot of Christians misunderstand the purpose of spiritual gifts, which is why Paul wrote this letter to the Corinthians and why we need to clarify any area of misunderstanding.

In the following chapter we shall take a look at a few misconceptions that people have about the gifts of the Holy Spirit.

Chapter 4

MISUNDERSTANDINGS OF THE GIFTS

There are many misunderstandings that people have about the gifts of the Holy Spirit, but we are going to look closely at just three of these misconceptions in this chapter.

Misunderstanding 1 – Gifts are given to us as a reward for our spirituality

The gifts of the Holy Spirit do not in any way determine how spiritual the person operating them is. We need to remember that they are gifts and are given to believers at the prerogative of the Holy Spirit, not as a result of anything the receiver has done or because they are deserving of it. Prior to becoming a king, Saul had a foretaste of a gift of the Holy Spirit such that people who saw him operating in this gift thought he had become a prophet.

"When you arrive at Gibeah of God, where the garrison of the Philistines is located, you will meet a band of prophets coming down from the place of worship. They will be playing a harp, a tambourine, a flute, and a lyre, and they will be prophesying. At that time the Spirit of the Lord will come powerfully upon you, and you will prophesy with them. You will be changed into a different person. After these signs take place, do what must be done, for God is with you. 1 Samuel 10:5–7

As Saul turned and started to leave, God gave him a new heart, and all Samuel's signs were fulfilled that day. When Saul and his servant arrived at Gibeah, they saw a group of prophets coming toward them. Then the Spirit of God came powerfully upon Saul, and he, too, began to prophesy. When those who knew Saul heard about it, they exclaimed, "What? Is even Saul a prophet? How did the son of Kish become a prophet?"

And one of those standing there said, "Can anyone become a prophet, no matter who his father is?" So that is the origin of the saying "Is even Saul a prophet?" 1 Samuel 10:9–12

Within what could not be more than a few hours, Saul was endowed with a gift of the Holy Spirit (see verse 6), much to the surprise of the people who saw him operate in this gift (see verses 9–12). The decision to endow Saul with this gift was entirely God's and Saul had not done anything to qualify for it. Furthermore, the fact that he was endowed with the gift did not suddenly make him bigger or better than anyone else.

It is therefore sad when believers rate themselves or other Christian according to the gifts God has given them, especially if they operate the 'power gifts' (healing, miracles, etc.), or when in some Christian circles believers are seen as "big men" or "big women" of God and placed in hierarchical levels based on the type of gifts they operate. This cannot be right as these gifts are given by God for us believers to use for the overall benefit of the church.

> A spiritual gift is given to each of us so we can help each other. 1 Corinthians 12:7

Misunderstanding 2 – we determine what spiritual gifts we receive

Even though in verse 31 of 1 Corinthians 12, Paul encouraged believers to "… earnestly desire the most helpful gifts", it is still the prerogative of the Holy Spirit to determine the type of gift He gives and whether or not to give any.

The Holy Spirit knows what every individual Christian can manage and as such distributes gifts in line with each person's ability.

While Jesus did not speak specifically about spiritual gifts in Matthew 25, I believe we can apply His teachings in this respect.

"Again, the Kingdom of Heaven can be illustrated by the story of a man going on a long trip. He called together his servants and entrusted his money to them while he was gone. He gave five bags of silver to one, two bags of silver to another, and one bag of silver to the last—dividing it in proportion to their abilities. He then left on his trip. Matthew 25: 14–15

As illustrated in Jesus' story, where money was entrusted to servants in proportion to their abilities, gifts of the Spirit are given to us in proportion to what each one of us can handle or in line with our abilities as predetermined by the

Holy Spirit. We should therefore graciously operate these gifts, ensuring that we do not get puffed up, remembering that we are only vessels (believers to whom the gift has been bestowed) through which God expresses His grace.

In his grace, God has given us different gifts for doing certain things well. So if God has given you the ability to prophesy, speak out with as much faith as God has given you. Romans 12:6

Misunderstanding 3 – Our spiritual gifts indicate our level of importance within the Body of Christ

Closely related to the issue of spirituality explained under Misunderstanding 1 is this issue of importance. Some believers think that the more gifts you have and the more visible your gifts are, the more important you are or must be.

Paul clearly debunked this notion while addressing the Corinthian Christians. As Christians we all belong to one body (the Body of Christ) and just as different parts of the body play different roles but still complement each other, each believer should make use of the individual gifts they possess to complement the ministries of other believers.

The human body has many parts, but the many parts make up one whole body. So it is with the body of Christ. Some of us are Jews, some are Gentiles, some are slaves, and some are free. But we have all been baptised into one body by one Spirit, and we all share the same Spirit.

Yes, the body has many different parts, not just one part. If the foot says, "I am not a part of the body because I am not a hand," that does not make it any less a part of the body. And if the ear says, "I am not part of the body because I am not an eye," would that make it any less a part of the body? If the whole body were an eye, how would you hear? Or if your whole body were an ear, how would you smell anything?

But our bodies have many parts, and God has put each part just where he wants it. How strange a body would be if it had only one part! Yes, there are many parts, but only one body. The eye can never say to the hand, "I don't need you." The head can't say to the feet, "I don't need you." 1 Corinthians 12:12–21

Paul furthermore explained that being a lowly part of the body does not amount to being less important.

In fact, some parts of the body that seem weakest and least important are actually the most necessary. And the parts we regard as less honourable are those we clothe with the greatest care. So we carefully protect those parts that should not be seen, while the more honourable parts do not require this special care. So God has put the body together such that extra honour and care are given to those parts that have less dignity. This makes for harmony among the members, so that all the members care for each other. If one part suffers, all the parts suffer with it, and if one part is honoured, all the parts are glad. 1 Corinthians 12:22–26

We must therefore be careful not to base our judgement of spiritual things on human reasoning; our duty is to "… care for each other".

It is most unfortunate that in a lot of churches (Body of Christ) today, people are rated based on how spiritually gifted we think they are. We all are vessels through which God operates His gifts so we must learn to honour the giver rather than the vessel. The vessels are meant to be channels of blessings; no wonder Paul was determined to show the Corinthian Christians "the most excellent way" or the best way of all:

So you should earnestly desire the most helpful gifts. But now let me show you a way of life that is best of all.
1 Corinthians 12:31

Chapter 5

IF I COULD SPEAK ALL
THE LANGUAGES OF THE
EARTH

I am sure anyone who has experienced the operations of any of the spiritual gifts will agree that they are very extraordinary, as these gifts enable ordinary people to do things extraordinarily. Paul the apostle described it this way:

> *In his grace, God has given us different gifts for doing certain things well. So if God has given you the ability to prophesy, speak out with as much faith as God has given you. If your gift is serving others, serve them well. If you are a teacher, teach well. If your gift is to encourage others, be encouraging. If it is giving, give generously. If God has given you leadership ability, take the responsibility seriously. And if you have a gift for showing kindness to others, do it gladly.* Romans 12:6–8

Whilst these gifts are great, there is always the possibility of abuse, particularly where the vessels (believers to whom the gifts have been bestowed) are immature and so have not fully grasped the purpose for which the Holy Spirit has endowed them with the gift.

The following story in the Book of Acts will help us shed some light on the kind of immature vessels that can misuse or abuse these gifts.

Philip the evangelist had done a great work in the city of Samaria, leading to the salvation of many citizens of the region. When Simon (who used to be a sorcerer but became a believer and was baptised by immersion) of Samaria saw Peter operate a gift of the Spirit, he demonstrated his misunderstanding of the purpose of the gift as well as his immaturity by offering Peter money in order to buy the ability to do the same. Peter rebuked him for his action.

When Simon saw that the Spirit was given when the apostles laid their hands on people, he offered them money to buy this power. "Let me have this power, too," he exclaimed, "so that when I lay my hands on people, they will receive the Holy Spirit!"

But Peter replied, "May your money be destroyed with you for thinking God's gift can be bought! You can have no part in this, for your heart is not right with God. Repent of your wickedness and pray to the Lord. Perhaps he will forgive your evil thoughts, for I can see that you are full of bitter jealousy and are held captive by sin."

"Pray to the Lord for me," Simon exclaimed, "that these terrible things you've said won't happen to me!"
Acts 8:18–24

Peter recognised Simon's immaturity, lack of character and the potential danger in bestowing any gift(s) on him prior to his growth into maturity, and therefore urged Simon to repent.

Unfortunately, there are many believers in our churches today who are endowed with one gift or another but have either forgotten the purpose for which they were endowed or are lacking in character, and so they misuse the gifts that have been bestowed upon them.

Isn't it sad when you see believers clearly endowed with extraordinary gifts, who have been elevated into leadership positions in their various ministries, but are rude to people and mistreat those who have been put in their charge? It is always difficult to reconcile their spiritual gifting with their poor relational ability.

It therefore does not matter how gifted and revered we are, and it does not matter what extraordinary things we are able to accomplish with our gifts, if we have not added one essential attribute: LOVE.

> *If I could speak all the languages of earth and of angels, but didn't love others, I would only be a noisy gong or a clanging cymbal. If I had the gift of prophecy, and if I understood all of God's secret plans and possessed all knowledge, and if I had such faith that I could move mountains, but didn't love others, I would be nothing. If I gave everything I have to the poor and even sacrificed my body, I could boast about it; but if I didn't love others, I would have gained nothing.* 1 Corinthians 13:1–3

One more thing to note is that every gift we are endowed with and express will only be useful on this side of eternity; none of them will last beyond the earth. If we don't use them for the purpose for which they have been given to us, which is to bless and uplift people here on earth, they will not be useful to us in heaven.

> *Prophecy and speaking in unknown languages and special knowledge will become useless. But love will last forever!*
> 1 Corinthians 13:8

Chapter 6

THE MOST EXCELLENT WAY

According to the online Oxford Living Dictionaries, the word 'WAY' can either be defined as, "a method, style, or manner of doing something; an optional or alternative form of action"[1], or "a road, track, or path for travelling along"[2]. Both definitions can apply with respect to the title of this book and our current chapter.

When Paul the apostle used this phrase in his letter to the church in Corinth, he was not only presenting love as "the most excellent" method, style, or manner of living the Christian life, he also meant it as "the most excellent" road, track or path along which a Christian must travel.

Excellent of course means to be "extremely good; out-standing"[3]. The way of love is the extremely good path for a Christian to travel; it is the outstanding method, style, or manner of living the Christian life.

However, this must have been a challenge for the Corinthian Christians to grapple with. They had only just had the most amazing experience of their lives (being born again), and as if that was not enough, they were supernaturally endowed with gifts by the Holy Spirit. They must have felt on top of the world, they must have been on "cloud nine".

Now imagine how they must have felt when Paul said to them that it wouldn't matter what extraordinary things they were able to accomplish with all their gifts if they didn't add the essential attribute, LOVE.

Why is LOVE so special and why does it surpass any other way? We will seek to answer this very important question in the remaining pages of this book. But let us start by looking a bit more at Paul's message in context.

A spiritual gift is given to each of us so we can help each other. To one person the Spirit gives the ability to give wise advice; to another the same Spirit gives a message of special knowledge. The same Spirit gives great faith to

another, and to someone else the one Spirit gives the gift of healing. He gives one person the power to perform miracles, and another the ability to prophesy. He gives someone else the ability to discern whether a message is from the Spirit of God or from another spirit. Still another person is given the ability to speak in unknown languages, while another is given the ability to interpret what is being said. It is the one and only Spirit who distributes all these gifts. He alone decides which gift each person should have.
1 Corinthians 12:7–11

Are we all apostles? Are we all prophets? Are we all teachers? Do we all have the power to do miracles? Do we all have the gift of healing? Do we all have the ability to speak in unknown languages? Do we all have the ability to interpret unknown languages? Of course not! So you should earnestly desire the most helpful gifts.

But now let me show you a way of life that is best of all.
1 Corinthians 12:29–31

When we look closely at the gifts of the Spirit as explained by Paul in 1 Corinthians 12:7–11, we will see clearly that they depict power and ability.

I am sure many human beings (believers included) will ask, 'What can be better than having power and divine ability?' It must therefore have intrigued the Corinthian Christians greatly when Paul said that he wanted to show them a way that is more excellent than that of power and divine ability – The Most Excellent Way, "… a way of life that is best of all".

I personally cannot think of any other adjectives that could have described this new way of life any better than those Paul used to describe it – The Most Excellent Way, "… a way of life that is best of all".

The way that Paul wanted to show the Corinthian Christian, and indeed every other believer, greatly surpasses any other way they may have known or applied. It surpasses "our own selfish way"; it surpasses "our gifted way". It is the way of LOVE. It is the way of GOD.

It transcends every human wisdom and understanding and it rises above all our human emotions and vices, as it enables us to step into the realm of the supernatural. It is the way that enables forgiveness and so allows us to fulfil the old adage that says, "To err is human but to forgive is divine."

In the next chapter we shall carefully explore this amazing way of love – "The Most Excellent Way".

[1,2] Way. 2017. In en.oxforddictionaries.com. Retrieved November 9, 2017, from https://en.oxforddictionaries.com/definition/way

[3] Excellent. 2017. In en.oxforddictionaries.com. Retrieved November 9, 2017, from https://en.oxforddictionaries.com/definition/excellent

Chapter 7

LOVE (THE FRUIT OF THE SPIRIT)

In order to gain a better understanding of Paul's assertion to the Corinthians about "The Most Excellent Way", particularly as it regards the inferiority of the gifts when compared with love, we need to explore the difference between the gifts and the fruit of the Spirit (love being the main component of the fruit of the Spirit).

> *But the Holy Spirit produces this kind of fruit in our lives: love, joy, peace, patience, kindness, goodness, faithfulness, gentleness, and self-control. There is no law against these things!* Galatians 5:22–23

The first thing to note as mentioned in the last chapter is that the gifts of the Spirit depict ability. In contrast, however, the fruit of the Spirit expresses character. The ability displayed through the exercise of each gift should not be misunder-stood as the personal ability of a person exercising these gifts, but as the ability of the Holy Spirit who Himself is the giver of all gifts.

To further explain, I speak in tongues because the Holy Spirit gives me the divine ability to do so, and not because I have the personal ability to do so. I will never be able to speak in tongues apart from the Holy Spirit.

Unlike the gifts, the fruit of the Spirit does not manifest auto-matically. As the Holy Spirit prompts us in the right direction towards producing Godly character, each Christian must indi-vidually put in a corresponding level of effort into ensuring that such character is fully developed.

Like many other Christians I have always pondered on Paul's reason for referring to the "fruit" of the Spirit in the singular rather than the plural, seeing that he went on to enumerate a number of Godly virtues, i.e. love, joy, peace, patience, kindness, goodness, faithfulness, gentleness and self-control. I have, however, come to a conclusion over the years that the Holy Spirit produces in us one primary fruit (love) which in turn expresses itself through all the other virtues such as joy, peace, patience, kindness, goodness, faithfulness, gentleness and self-control.

It is in cultivating this amazing character of love and making it the road, track or path on which we travel in order to fulfil all our desires, goals, actions and ministries as children of God that we succeed in following "The Most Excellent Way".

In the following chapters, we will look more closely at the different ways through which this amazing fruit of love is expressed through the virtues listed above, but first let me go back to the delay I had in writing this book...

Chapter 8

LOVE IS PATIENT

Love is patient and kind... 1 Corinthians 13:4

In Paul's definition of love as recorded in 1 Corinthians 13, he started with two positive attributes of love or "what love is" (one of which we will be looking at in this chapter), and then went on to enumerate a host of things that love is not and what love will never do.

It might interest you to know that both attributes that describe what love is (patience and kindness) are attributes that describes the nature of God. It is no wonder then that in one of his epistles John the Beloved declared that God is love.

> *But anyone who does not love does not know God, for God is love.* 1 John 4:8

Moses described God's patience in the Book of Exodus as follows:

> *The Lord passed in front of Moses, calling out, "Yahweh! The Lord! The God of compassion and mercy! I am slow to anger and filled with unfailing love and faithfulness.* Exodus 34:6

I will always be grateful to God for His patience towards me in not keeping a record of my sin, and it is my prayer that through the help of His Holy Spirit I will learn to apply this grace to people around me.

> *LORD, if you kept a record of our sins, who, O Lord, could ever survive?* Psalm 130:3

Very early in my Christian life, I discovered that God had endowed me with the grace to teach and that through the power of His Holy Spirit I had received the gift of "teaching". Through this grace I have received deep insight into God's Word, with the ability to interpret deep things.

It has always been clear to me when this gift is in operation in my life that the abilities that I express during those moments are not mine but God's. I have also always been careful to return every glory to God in these situations.

I remember teaching on several occasions that as children of God we will never be able to claim that we are patient until we have experienced delay or challenges in important areas of our lives, and are able to genuinely smile through these delays and trials of our patience. James the apostle puts it a very interesting way:

> Dear brothers and sisters, when troubles of any kind come your way, consider it an opportunity for great joy. For you know that when your faith is tested, your endurance has a chance to grow. So let it grow, for when your endurance is fully developed, you will be perfect and complete, needing nothing.
> James 1:2–4

I don't know how many of us Christians (including those who have been in the Lord for a long time) can truly claim to rejoice when any kind of trouble comes our way. According to James, our patience (translated endurance in the New Living Translation [NLT]) "…has a chance to grow" and become "fully developed" when troubles come our way.

Without meaning to shower praises on myself, I can safely say that the area of patience is one that I more than most people around me have been thought to excel in – that is, until a series of incidents that occurred just a few years prior to writing this book. I have over the years learnt to smile through many trials and tribulations.

I can still picture in my mind the times when I have been cheated or maltreated and have responded with kind words or silence, having learnt from God's Word the benefit of both. In some of these instances a number of people around me had thought I was either cowardly or stupid to have accepted the things done to me without responding. In spite of whatever they may have thought, or how demeaning the situation may have felt, I had held on to God's words:

A gentle answer deflects anger, but harsh words make tempers flare. Proverbs 15:1

Dear friends, never take revenge. Leave that to the righteous anger of God. For the Scriptures say, "I will take revenge; I will pay them back," says the LORD. Romans 12:19

Having being a Christian for about 30 years, I have learnt not to take people's actions too seriously and also to leave matters to God. When therefore, following the incidents referred to earlier, I found myself expressing emotions that I thought were long dead, I knew I was far from being perfect and I needed the Lord to help me out.

I won't go into much detail as it may seem unfair on the other people involved, particularly as I also cannot fully exonerate myself in the matters that occurred. I have realised that no one is perfect and as we journey toward perfection we will realise that as children of God, we all have different areas of strength and also things that we value differ.

Having said all that, I felt angry and hurt, perhaps not because of the things done to me but because of the people involved, as they were not only brothers and sisters in Christ, but they were also people I held in high esteem.

Suffice it to say that although I made a conscious effort to forgive everyone concerned, I did not "count it all joy", neither did I "consider it an opportunity for great joy" (at least not at the time). I took drastic steps to stay as far away as possible from the people concerned. It also affected my ability to have any deep relationship with people because I was always wary of being hurt by them.

It may surprise you when I say that I now feel most grateful to God that I went through those experiences, as they have enabled me to re-evaluate my Christian life. I am now better able to view the "bigger picture" in most circumstances, with the understanding that sometimes God allows "hurt" in order to make us grow in endurance and become more perfect. Unfortunately, for hurt to happen, people have to be involved and many times these are people who are close to us and people that we love.

According to James, the troubles we experience in life are endurance tests. Passing each endurance test moves us up one level towards perfection. My experience was clearly a test that I did not pass straight away. In my final analysis, however, I am like the person who fought and ran away, but I am grateful to God that I am alive to "fight another day".

One main lesson I have learnt through my experience is that you can be right and wrong at the same time. As children of God, even when we are in the right our response to offence must always be from God's perspective. If we allow our emotions to overrun we will only be placing ourselves in a marking time position (not being able to move forward in life). I am glad to say that I now have so much incredible love in my heart for these my brothers and sisters, and as soon as the Holy Spirit enabled me to develop such love my life's gear was engaged in forward drive.

Why is the way of patience a more excellent way?

Unlike our own self-led way or our gifted way of living, patience has the ability to:

1. See the bigger picture. It sees far ahead into the future.
2. It rises above whatever form of evil is done against it.
3. It is always calm and peace-loving.
4. It is never vengeful as it recognises that vengeance belongs to God.
5. Is always forgiving and never keeps a record of wrongdoing.
6. It recognises the presence of God in every circumstance.
7. It recognises the fact that God has the final say in every human affair.

We find a great example of patience in the patriarch Joseph. Instead of being angry with his brothers for the evil done to him, he chose to forgive and comfort them, having recognised that their actions were utilised by God.

> *"I am Joseph!" he said to his brothers. "Is my father still alive?" But his brothers were speechless! They were stunned to realise that Joseph was standing there in front of them. "Please, come closer," he said to them. So they came closer. And he said again, "I am Joseph, your brother, whom you sold into slavery in Egypt. But don't be upset, and don't be angry with yourselves for selling me to this place. It was God who sent me here ahead of you to preserve your lives. This famine that has ravaged the land for two years will last five more years, and there will be neither ploughing nor harvesting. God has sent me ahead of you to keep you and your families alive and to preserve many survivors. So it was God who sent me here, not you! And he is the one who made me an adviser to Pharaoh—the manager of his entire palace and the governor of all Egypt.* Genesis 45:3–8

What an amazing display of patient love!

We require divine assistance in order to develop the fruit of patience and like Paul, I *"pray that you will be strengthened with all his glorious power so you will have all the endurance and patience you need..."* (Colossians 1:11).

Chapter 9

LOVE IS KIND

Kindness (generosity of spirit, friendliness and ability to show great respect for others) is such an amazing virtue for any human being to have. It is interesting that Paul seemed to have tied patience and kindness together in his letter to the Corinthians. This connection gives me the impetus to make the following assertion.

While it is inevitable for offences to occur, and though God allows these to happen in order to make us grow in endurance and become more perfect, having the fruit of kindness should mean that we as His children must not be responsible for offences.

First, I hear that there are divisions among you when you meet as a church, and to some extent I believe it. But, of course, there must be divisions among you so

that you who have God's approval will be recognised!
1 Corinthians 11:18–19

Jesus made clear through the following scripture the dangers of being responsible for offences:

"What sorrow awaits the world, because it tempts people to sin. Temptations are inevitable, but what sorrow awaits the person who does the tempting." Matthew 18:7

Let us move away from this issue of offences and focus more on the fruit of kindness. I have seen and experienced acts of kindness from Christians and non-Christians alike. I also understand the sheer joy that comes with being a beneficiary of kindness. Kindness as a fruit of the Spirit is perhaps a lot deeper than the sort of kindness that most people practise, as it goes the extra mile and does not use duty as an excuse for its lack of expression.

I have seen over the years of being a Christian that a number of believers get so carried away by their responsibilities and roles, or so engrossed with the use of their spiritual gifts, that kindness completely goes out of the window. As far as they are concerned they are serving the

Lord and nothing must get in the way, not even kindness.

Our Lord painted this picture for us through the popular story of the Good Samaritan. The priest and the Levite were too engrossed with their responsibilities and were not available to show kindness to a man in need.

Jesus replied with a story: "A Jewish man was travelling from Jerusalem down to Jericho, and he was attacked by bandits. They stripped him of his clothes, beat him up, and left him half dead beside the road.

"By chance a priest came along. But when he saw the man lying there, he crossed to the other side of the road and passed him by. A Temple assistant walked over and looked at him lying there, but he also passed by on the other side.

"Then a despised Samaritan came along, and when he saw the man, he felt compassion for him. Going over to him, the Samaritan soothed his wounds with olive oil and wine and bandaged them. Then he put the man on his own donkey and took him to an inn, where he took care of him. The next day he handed the innkeeper two

silver coins, telling him, 'Take care of this man. If his bill runs higher than this, I'll pay you the next time I'm here.'

"Now which of these three would you say was a neighbour to the man who was attacked by bandits?" Jesus asked.

The man replied, "The one who showed him mercy."

Then Jesus said, "Yes, now go and do the same."
Luke 10:30–37

Isn't it rather sad that over two thousand years after our Lord Jesus told this story, many believers would rather demonstrate how great they are through the display of their spiritual gifts than develop their character and excel in the fruit of kindness? His commandment in this scripture still stands: "*... now go and do the same*".

Our Lord Jesus is the epitome of kindness. Most, if not all, of His miracles came out of a compassionate heart. One particular incidence that demonstrates His kindness involved the woman caught in the act of adultery. It also distinguishes him from the religious people of His time, who were more concerned about ticking the box of their religion than placing value on human life. Jesus demonstrated through His actions how kindness is part of "The Most Excellent Way".

Jesus returned to the Mount of Olives, but early the next morning he was back again at the Temple. A crowd soon gathered, and he sat down and taught them. As he was speaking, the teachers of religious law and the Pharisees brought a woman who had been caught in the act of adultery. They put her in front of the crowd.

"Teacher," they said to Jesus, "this woman was caught in the act of adultery. The law of Moses says to stone her. What do you say?"

They were trying to trap him into saying something they could use against him, but Jesus stooped down and wrote in the dust with his finger. They kept demanding an answer, so he stood up again and said, "All right, but let the one who has never sinned throw the first stone!" Then he stooped down again and wrote in the dust.

When the accusers heard this, they slipped away one by one, beginning with the oldest, until only Jesus was left in the middle of the crowd with the woman. Then Jesus stood up again and said to the woman, "Where are your accusers? Didn't even one of them condemn you?"

"No, Lord," she said.

And Jesus said, "Neither do I. Go and sin no more."
John 8:1–11

This story has never ceased to amaze me, as it demonstrates how God is more willing to forgive human beings than we are prepared to forgive each other. Sadly, in a lot of Christian gatherings today, there are many who like the teachers of religious law and the Pharisees have turned themselves into religious police, seeking out offenders that need to be stoned. And when you look closely at their own lives, there are deeper issues of sin which may not be immediately obvious. Kindness is not vindictive, rather it is an act of love that *"… covers a multitude of sins"* (1 Peter 4:8).

In another instance, in spite of opposition from the religious leaders of His time, Jesus showed kindness to a sick woman who had been bound by Satan for several years. Unlike these leaders, He did not use the law or religion as an excuse for not showing kindness.

One Sabbath day as Jesus was teaching in a synagogue, he saw a woman who had been crippled by an evil spirit. She had been bent double for eighteen years and was unable to stand up straight. When Jesus saw her, he called her over and said, "Dear woman, you are healed of your sickness!" Then he touched her, and instantly she could stand straight. How she praised God!

But the leader in charge of the synagogue was indignant that Jesus had healed her on the Sabbath day. "There are six days of the week for working," he said to the crowd. "Come on those days to be healed, not on the Sabbath."

But the Lord replied, "You hypocrites! Each of you works on the Sabbath day! Don't you untie your ox or your donkey from its stall on the Sabbath and lead it out for water? This dear woman, a daughter of Abraham, has been held in bondage by Satan for eighteen years. Isn't it right that she be released, even on the Sabbath?"

This shamed his enemies, but all the people rejoiced at the wonderful things he did.
Luke 13:10–17

We can see from this passage that Holy Spirit-inspired acts of kindness glorify God, shame the enemy and bring great joy to people.

Why is the way of kindness a more excellent way?

Unlike our own self-led way or our gifted way of living, kindness has the ability to:

1. Feel the pain and need of others. Philippians 2:4
2. Become sensitive to the emotional needs of others. Ephesians 4:29
3. Display a generous spirit without seeking any reward. Luke 6:35
4. Seeks to serve rather than to be served. Hebrews 6:10
5. Show sympathy. Isaiah 58:6–7
6. Show forgiveness. Ephesians 4:32
7. Go the extra mile for others. Philippians 2:3–4

At the beginning of this chapter we looked at 1 Corinthians 11:18–19 where Paul was addressing the divisions reported to have existed among the Corinthian Christians. As we close this chapter I would like us to take a closer look at some more verses in this passage where Paul was speaking to the church about Holy Communion or Eucharist.

But in the following instructions, I cannot praise you. For it sounds as if more harm than good is done when you meet together. First, I hear that there are divisions among you when you meet as a church, and to some extent I believe it. But, of course, there must be divisions among you so that you who have God's approval will be recognised!

When you meet together, you are not really interested in the Lord's Supper. For some of you hurry to eat your own meal without sharing with others. As a result, some go hungry while others get drunk. What? Don't you have your own homes for eating and drinking? Or do you really want to disgrace God's church and shame the poor? What am I supposed to say? Do you want me to praise you? Well, I certainly will not praise you for this!

For I pass on to you what I received from the Lord himself. On the night when he was betrayed, the Lord Jesus took some bread and gave thanks to God for it. Then he broke it in pieces and said, "This is my body, which is given for you. Do this in remembrance of me." In the same way, he took the cup of wine after supper, saying, "This cup is the new covenant between God and his people—an agreement confirmed with my blood. Do this in remembrance of me as often as you drink it." For every time you eat this bread and drink this cup, you are announcing the Lord's death until he comes again.

So anyone who eats this bread or drinks this cup of the Lord unworthily is guilty of sinning against the body and blood of the Lord. That is why you should examine yourself before eating the bread and drinking the cup. For if you eat the bread or drink the cup without honouring the body of Christ, you are eating and drinking God's judgment upon yourself. That is why many of you are weak and sick and some have even died.

But if we would examine ourselves, we would not be judged by God in this way. Yet when we are judged by the Lord, we are being disciplined so that we will not be condemned along with the world. 1 Corinthians 11:17–32

If you look closely at this passage, you will discover that every lack of kindness and generosity in the church amounts to bringing disgrace to God's church and shame to the poor.

What? Don't you have your own homes for eating and drinking? Or do you really want to disgrace God's church and shame the poor? What am I supposed to say? Do you want me to praise you? Well, I certainly will not praise you for this! 1 Corinthians 11:22

Even more than these, it amounts to dishonouring the Lord's body (the Church) an act that will be severely punished if not repented of.

So anyone who eats this bread or drinks this cup of the Lord unworthily is guilty of sinning against the body and blood of the Lord. That is why you should examine yourself before eating the bread and drinking the cup. For if you eat the bread or drink the cup without honouring the body of Christ, you are eating and drinking God's judgment upon yourself. That is why many of you are weak and sick and some have even died. 1 Corinthians 11:27–30

We dishonour the Lord's body whenever we act selfishly and refuse to consider other members of His body. We dishonour the Lord's body when we trample on other believers who are lowlier than we are. The Church as a whole needs to repent in order to obtain God's mercy.

But if we would examine ourselves, we would not be judged by God in this way. Yet when we are judged by the Lord, we are being disciplined so that we will not be condemned along with the world. 1 Corinthians 11:31–32

It is my prayer that God will fill us all with *"... more and more mercy, peace, and love"* (Jude 1:2). Amen.

As children of God, He expects us to represent Him in demonstrating kindness to all around us, particularly to those who are fellow believers.

So let's not get tired of doing what is good. At just the right time we will reap a harvest of blessing if we don't give up. Therefore, whenever we have the opportunity, we should do good to everyone – especially to those in the family of faith. Galatians 6:9–10

Chapter 10

LOVE IS NOT JEALOUS OR BOASTFUL OR PROUD OR RUDE

In the last two chapters, we looked at two extraordinary expressions of love. We are now moving on to look at what love is not.

One scripture that has captivated me a lot as a believer is James 1:22–25, as I am constantly reminded of these verses when I am getting ready to leave home in the morning, possibly after shaving. If while looking in the mirror, I discover a lump of hair that I have left unshaved, I am sure that I will quickly do something about it. It is highly unlikely that I will leave home without ensuring that I am looking nice and perfectly normal (unless of course I am participating in a bad hair day event!).

But don't just listen to God's word. You must do what it says. Otherwise, you are only fooling yourselves. For if you listen to the word and don't obey, it is like glancing at your face in a mirror. You see yourself, walk away, and forget what you look like. But if you look carefully into the perfect law that sets you free, and if you do what it says and don't forget what you heard, then God will bless you for doing it. James 1:22–25

I have introduced this scripture here because as we look closely at what love is not, it is essential for us to look into the mirror of God's Word to ensure that we do not match any of the descriptions used by Paul. If however we do, we need to do the same thing we would do if we were in front of a mirror – make whatever adjustment is needed in order to ensure that we look alright.

Love is not Jealous

Jealousy is a negative emotion that occurs when a person envies another because of what they have, and would do their utmost to acquire it.

The first evidence of jealousy occurred right at the beginning of the Bible just after creation. Abel had received God's commendation and blessing for doing the right thing and his brother Cain became jealous to the extent that he killed him.

> When it was time for the harvest, Cain presented some of his crops as a gift to the Lord. Abel also brought a gift—the best portions of the firstborn lambs from his flock. The Lord accepted Abel and his gift, but he did not accept Cain and his gift. This made Cain very angry, and he looked dejected.

> "Why are you so angry?" the Lord asked Cain. "Why do you look so dejected? You will be accepted if you do what is right. But if you refuse to do what is right, then watch out! Sin is crouching at the door, eager to control you. But you must subdue it and be its master."

> One day Cain suggested to his brother, "Let's go out into the fields." And while they were in the field, Cain attacked his brother, Abel, and killed him. Genesis 4:3–8

Instead of amending his ways and doing what is right in order to obtain God's blessing, Cain became jealous of his brother and in spite of God's warning, he committed murder. Sadly, there is still a lot of murder being carried out in people's hearts – and physically – today as a result of envy.

If you are never content with what you have, but always desire what belongs to others, or if you dislike them because you think they have a better life than you, you need to look at the mirror of God's Word and repent, as you are not acting in love. The Lord is saying to you like He did to Cain:

> *"Why are you so angry?" the Lord asked Cain. "Why do you look so dejected? You will be accepted if you do what is right. But if you refuse to do what is right, then watch out! Sin is crouching at the door, eager to control you. But you must subdue it and be its master."*
> Genesis 4:6-7

Love is not Boastful or Proud or Rude

All these listed vices – boastfulness, pride and rudeness – are closely related, with one leading on to another. While jealousy occurs as a result of envy and wanting to have what belongs to another, boastfulness, pride and rudeness occur as a result of an overestimation of one's self and possessions, resulting in self-adulation and looking down on others.

When a person becomes proud because of their estimation of themselves or because of their achievements and possessions, they may then also become boastful, thinking that these achievements, etc. are a result of their own effort and intelligence. In their boastfulness, they look down on and treat others with rudeness.

All three vices (boastfulness, pride and rudeness) express insensitivity towards God and others, and as children of God we must steer clear of them because they are detested by God to the extent that He *"opposes the proud but gives grace to the humble"* (James 4:6). There are several examples of such displays of pride in the Bible, each ending disastrously for the proud person. A few examples and relevant passages are listed below:

1. Pharaoh's pride against God – Exodus 5:2
2. Goliath's pride against David and the people of Israel – 1 Samuel 17:41–42
3. Nebuchadnezzar's self-adulation – Daniel 4:30
4. Peter's pride and boastfulness – Matthew 26:33–35

And there are many more. The passage I would like us to explore is the one in Luke 18 that relates to a Pharisee and a

63

Tax Collector, because if care is not taken, when as believers we look into the mirror of God's Word, we may find ourselves looking like the Pharisee in this passage:

> *Then Jesus told this story to some who had great confidence in their own righteousness and scorned everyone else: "Two men went to the Temple to pray. One was a Pharisee, and the other was a despised tax collector. The Pharisee stood by himself and prayed this prayer: 'I thank you, God, that I am not like other people— cheaters, sinners, adulterers. I'm certainly not like that tax collector! I fast twice a week, and I give you a tenth of my income.'*

> *"But the tax collector stood at a distance and dared not even lift his eyes to heaven as he prayed. Instead, he beat his chest in sorrow, saying, 'O God, be merciful to me, for I am a sinner.' I tell you, this sinner, not the Pharisee, returned home justified before God. For those who exalt themselves will be humbled, and those who humble them-selves will be exalted." Luke 18:9–14*

The Pharisee clearly did not act in love as he displayed all forms of insensitivity (boastfulness, pride and rudeness) in this text. He prided himself on his self-righteousness and boasted about his acts of righteousness in fasting and tithing, amongst others. He then acted rudely by belittling the tax collector, not minding the effect of his attitude on others.

In order to walk successfully through this excellent way of love we must never forget firstly that our salvation which gave rise to our righteousness is a gift from God.

> *God saved you by his grace when you believed. And you can't take credit for this; it is a gift from God. Salvation is not a reward for the good things we have done, so none of us can boast about it.* Ephesians 2:8–9

Moreover, we need to remind ourselves that following our salvation, everything we have has been loaned to us by God, so we cannot boast about these things.

> *For what gives you the right to make such a judgment? What do you have that God hasn't given you? And if everything you have is from God, why boast as though it were not a gift?* 1 Corinthians 4:7

Chapter 11

LOVE DOES NOT DEMAND ITS OWN WAY.

IT IS NOT IRRITABLE, AND IT KEEPS NO RECORD OF BEING WRONGED.

Having established what love is not, we move forward to look at how love does not express itself. All three vices being considered in this chapter reflect acts of childishness, and so are not expressions of love as true love expresses itself through acts of maturity.

As I mentioned in the previous two chapters, if we look into the mirror of God's Word and the image we see looks in any way like the three vices described, we can conclude that we are not walking in true love. We will therefore need to make all necessary amendments until the image reflected back to us is love.

Love... does not demand its own way

Another translation of the Bible puts it this way: "... it is not self-seeking" (NIV). How often have you heard this expression used, "My way or the highway"? Even though people who use this expression want to demonstrate their strength, the expression and the attitude that accompanies it reveals weakness and immaturity.

I have seen this verse of scripture used several times in Christian wedding ceremonies, when the couple and congregation are being addressed after the solemnisation. This link to weddings may almost make one think that not demanding one's way only relates to marriages. While it is essential for couples who want to have long-lasting and successful marriages to apply this principle, it cuts across all forms of relationships. For any relationship to thrive there has to be some element of give as well as take.

Love ultimately seeks the will of God as it knows that the will of God is always perfect, and no other person demonstrates this more perfectly than our Lord and Saviour Jesus Himself. Even when He realised that doing the will of the Father meant pain and suffering, He submitted Himself to it. He did not demand His own way.

> *He walked away, about a stone's throw, and knelt down and prayed, "Father, if you are willing, please take this cup of suffering away from me. Yet I want your will to be done, not mine." Then an angel from heaven appeared and strengthened him. He prayed more fervently, and he was in such agony of spirit that his sweat fell to the ground like great drops of blood.* Luke 22:41–44

It is no wonder then that God was pleased with Him, giving Him a name that is above all names. Paul the apostle encourages us as believers to have this same attitude that Christ displayed. It is a great attitude of love expressed through maturity, sacrifice and humility.

> *You must have the same attitude that Christ Jesus had.*

> *Though he was God, he did not think of equality with God as something to cling to. Instead, he gave up his divine privileges; he took the humble position of a slave and*

was born as a human being. When he appeared in human form, he humbled himself in obedience to God and died a criminal's death on a cross. Therefore, God elevated him to the place of highest honour and gave him the name above all other names, that at the name of Jesus every knee should bow, in heaven and on earth and under the earth, and every tongue declare that Jesus Christ is Lord, to the glory of God the Father. Philippians 2:5–11

It is my prayer that we will receive the grace to express the image of God in this respect in Jesus' name.

Love is not irritable

It is good to have and maintain very high standards, but if such high standards make us touchy and bad-tempered, we aren't expressing God's loving image.

While I wouldn't consider myself to be an ill-tempered person, I do like things to be done to some exacting standards. I have over the past few months been ensuring that my demand for high standards does not translate in any way into ill-temper or petulance when people around me do not meet my standards.

The solution to this issue of irritability, like all the other vices mentioned in this chapter, can be found in the application of the 'Golden Rule', which is: *"Do to others whatever you would like them to do to you..."* Matthew 7:12.

Several years ago, after I became a Christian, I soon discovered that many believers within the Body complain about the treatment they receive from other believers, particularly those in higher positions (please note that complaining about unpalatable circumstances is not new; we find examples in the Bible – see Acts 6:1–7). It surprised me greatly when, after some years, those who complained found themselves in similar positions and they did exactly the same things they complained about to people under them.

Having observed these sorts of behaviour several times over, and having experienced some negative treatments myself, I made a vow long ago that I will not treat people in any way that I do not like being treated. I believe that every Christian, particularly those who are in a position of authority, must make a conscious effort to live by the Golden Rule.

We must remember that while godly human mentors are good, they sometimes have flaws in their own lives, so Christ must be our standard, not our human mentors. Even when Paul encouraged the Corinthian Christians to imitate him, it was only to the extent that he himself imitated Christ.

> *And you should imitate me, just as I imitate Christ.*
> 1 Corinthians 11:1

Another area where believers might become irritable is in the area of reaching out to others. Oftentimes leaders, and particularly their aides, become irritated when they perceive that they are being bothered with trivial matters. I have seen people being shoved away or even spoken to rudely by aides of Christian leaders because in their opinion these people are being a bother. Jesus' disciples behaved in exactly the same way but were quickly corrected by their master:

> *One day some parents brought their children to Jesus so he could lay his hands on them and pray for them. But the disciples scolded the parents for bothering him.*
>
> *But Jesus said, "Let the children come to me. Don't stop them! For the Kingdom of Heaven belongs to those who are like these children." And he placed his hands on their heads and blessed them before he left.* Matthew 19:13–15

I do appreciate the fact that as human beings we may not be able to meet all the needs of people who come to us and that there is only so much we can do for people, it is however important that in communicating this we must do so kindly. We should treat them just as we would expect to be treated if we found ourselves in similar situations.

Interestingly, when we analyse what Jesus meant when He said that the Kingdom of Heaven belongs to those who are like these children, we find that it relates closely to our next point of discussion (love keeps no record of being wronged). This is because children very quickly forget being wronged; they forgive their offending friends and move on.

Love Keeps no Record of Being Wronged

For his unfailing love toward those who fear him is as great as the height of the heavens above the earth. He has removed our sins as far from us as the east is from the west. Psalm 103:11–12

God will never ask us to do anything that He Himself is not prepared to do for us. I am sure that I will not be too far from the truth if I say that forgetting the wrong done to us by others is a lot more challenging to most human beings than forgiving it. Unlike us, whenever God forgives, He "wipes the slate clean" and goes to a great length to separate us from our sin (as far as the east is from the west), so that whenever He looks at us He sees us in the light of His forgiveness, as if we had never sinned before.

In the first chapter of this book, I spoke briefly about an incident that happened to me a few years prior to writing this book. I made further mention of this in the eighth chapter while dealing with the issue of patience, as I realised that the incidence brought out in me emotions that I felt were no longer present in my life.

As mentioned in the eighth chapter, even though I had forgiven all the people concerned in my heart, I hadn't forgotten what was done to me. While I never reacted to any of the people involved in accordance with my hurt, it prevented me from having any close relationship(s) with people, until God opened my eyes to see the bigger picture.

I remembered that nothing could ever happen to me unless God allows it, and that He causes all things to work together for my good. With the knowledge that all my experiences are within God's plan for my life, I determined in my heart that I was going to forget whatever wrong was done to me (please note, as stated previously, that I do not claim to be without any blame in the matter).

I immediately felt great peace and I knew within me that I had just received the grace to march forward; I knew that my season had changed.

The decision about whether or not to keep records of wrong is a matter of choice. God forgives us and forgets all our wrong-doing not because He is unintelligent and does not have the capacity to remember, but because of His unfailing love for us. He makes a conscious and determined decision to forget our sins. He "... *removed our sins as far from us as the east is from the west*" (Psalm 103:12).

If you are reading this book and have been offended by people so often that you have decided not to forget what they have done to you, I would encourage you to change your mind. Make a decision to forgive and be determined not to keep a record of their offences against you. If you genuinely do this, I can assure you that you will experience a divine release and begin to experience true progress in your life.

Chapter 12

LOVE DOES NOT REJOICE
ABOUT INJUSTICE...

Love Does Not Rejoice About Injustice

How do you respond when something evil happens to your oppressor or someone who clearly does not like you? Would you consider it an opportunity to gloat and celebrate the downfall of your enemy or would you feel sympathetic about their plight?

In asking the above questions, I have presumed that you are not directly responsible for the evil experienced by your oppressor; however, isn't there an actual possibility that there are children of God who can plan to and do inflict evil on those who oppress them? Assuming the answer is yes, wouldn't they then rejoice when they realise that their evil plan(s) has come to fruition?

The NLT translation of 1 Corinthians 13:6 uses the word "injustice". This might suggest that when evil things happen to bad people it may be alright to rejoice because that will be justice. This is why I prefer some of the other translations here, where words like evil, wrongdoing, iniquity and unrighteousness are used in place of injustice. It is my firm belief that love will never rejoice when any of these (evil, wrongdoing, iniquity and unrighteousness) is experienced by any fellow human being, whether they are good or bad, nice or unpleasant.

Someone who demonstrated this attitude of love in the Bible was David. In 2 Samuel 18, the Bible records that even though David was clearly wronged by his son Absalom, he did not rejoice at his death but mourned bitterly because of it. Well, okay, I do agree that Absalom was David's son so that might explain his reaction, but that doesn't apply in the case of David's reaction to King Saul's death.

Saul had tried several times to kill David, yet when Saul died David refused to rejoice and instead mourned his death:

David and his men tore their clothes in sorrow when they heard the news. They mourned and wept and fasted all day for Saul and his son Jonathan,

and for the Lord's army and the nation of Israel,
because they had died by the sword that day.
2 Samuel 1:11–12

The Bible clearly warns us against rejoicing at the misfortune of our enemies, as doing so arouses God's displeasure.

Don't rejoice when your enemies fall; don't be happy when
they stumble. For the LORD will be displeased with you
and will turn his anger away from them. Proverbs 24:17–18

David clearly understood the dangers of gloating over the misfortune of his enemies; he understood the need to walk along the most excellent way of love.

It is rather sad that some supposed churches today actually encourage their members to pray for evil to happen to their enemies and for them to die. This completely negates the teachings of our Lord and Saviour Jesus Christ.

There is one particular teaching of Christ in Matthew 5:43–48 that has always intrigued me. This instruction is very important for anyone who claims to be a child of God, as practising it ascertains the truth about whether or not we are truly children of God:

"You have heard the law that says, 'Love your neighbour' and hate your enemy. But I say, love your enemies! Pray for those who persecute you! **In that way, you will be acting as true children of your Father in heaven.** *For he gives his sunlight to both the evil and the good, and he sends rain on the just and the unjust alike. If you love only those who love you, what reward is there for that? Even corrupt tax collectors do that much. If you are kind only to your friends, how are you different from anyone else? Even pagans do that. But you are to be perfect, even as your Father in heaven is perfect.*

Love rejoices when truth wins

If we cannot rejoice over the misfortune(s) of our enemies, what then can we rejoice over? The answer is very clear from 1 Corinthians 13:6 – the prevalence of TRUTH.

Paul's declaration that love rejoices "whenever the truth wins out" suggests a duel or competition between truth and injustice (evil, falsehood). If we look around us on a daily basis we will see this duel (competition, conflict) acted out and displayed over and over again in the various activities we either observe or participate in.

One clear example of love rejoicing when truth wins can be seen in the story of Daniel. His colleagues had conspired against him and tried to get him killed because of his faith in God and their jealousy. The unsuspecting king had signed a law, before he realised that he had been tricked, that would see Daniel killed:

Darius the Mede decided to divide the kingdom into 120 provinces, and he appointed a high officer to rule over each province. The king also chose Daniel and two others as administrators to supervise the high officers and protect the king's interests. Daniel soon proved himself more capable than all the other administrators and high officers. Because of Daniel's great ability, the king made plans to place him over the entire empire.

Then the other administrators and high officers began searching for some fault in the way Daniel was handling government affairs, but they couldn't find anything to criticize or condemn. He was faithful, always responsible, and completely trustworthy. So they concluded, "Our only chance of finding grounds for accusing Daniel will be in connection with the rules of his religion."

So the administrators and high officers went to the king and said, "Long live King Darius! ⁷ We are all in agreement— we administrators, officials, high officers, advisers, and governors—that the king should make a law that will be strictly enforced. Give orders that for the next thirty days any person who prays to anyone, divine or human— except to you, Your Majesty—will be thrown into the den of lions. And now, Your Majesty, issue and sign this law so it cannot be changed, an official law of the Medes and Persians that cannot be revoked." So King Darius signed the law.
Daniel 6:1–9

Daniel's enemies succeeded in getting their way. Daniel remained faithful to God and continued to pray, so he was arrested and thrown into the lion's den. Darius demonstrated true love in two respects:

1. Even though he could not repeal the law, he did not rejoice over the injustice done to Daniel:

   Then they told the king, "That man Daniel, one of the captives from Judah, is ignoring you and your law. He still prays to his God three times a day."

Hearing this, the king was deeply troubled, and he tried to think of a way to save Daniel. He spent the rest of the day looking for a way to get Daniel out of this predicament.

In the evening the men went together to the king and said, "Your Majesty, you know that according to the law of the Medes and the Persians, no law that the king signs can be changed."

So at last the king gave orders for Daniel to be arrested and thrown into the den of lions. The king said to him, "May your God, whom you serve so faithfully, rescue you."
Daniel 6:13–16

2. Secondly, Darius rejoiced when TRUTH prevailed. He had prayed that Daniel's God would deliver him, and when this happened, Darius rejoiced:

Then the king returned to his palace and spent the night fasting. He refused his usual entertainment and couldn't sleep at all that night.

Very early the next morning, the king got up and hurried out to the lions' den. When he got there, he called out in anguish, "Daniel, servant of the living God! Was your God, whom you serve so faithfully, able to rescue you from the lions?"

Daniel answered, "Long live the king! My God sent his angel to shut the lions' mouths so that they would not hurt me, for I have been found innocent in his sight. And I have not wronged you, Your Majesty."

The king was overjoyed and ordered that Daniel be lifted from the den. Not a scratch was found on him, for he had trusted in his God. Daniel 6:18–23

Darius, unlike many of Israel and Judah's kings prior to their exile, demonstrated excellence in his love. In 1 Kings 21, for example, King Ahab rejoiced at the death of Naboth as this gave him the opportunity to take over Naboth's vineyard.

The real test of love for you and me in every situation that we experience, participate in or are confronted with, is in how we respond to the outcome of each experience. Will we insist on the truth and rejoice in it, even when it is at our own expense, or will we take sides with falsehood because it is going to be to our advantage?

Many of the 'Christian' nations of the world that profited from slavery and the slave trade for about four centuries struggled to put an end to it. When eventually it was abolished in some nations, not all so-called 'Christians' rejoiced. In fact, many protested and some still do centuries later, because the end of slavery and the injustices that accompanied it also meant an end to their profiteering and misuse of their fellow human beings.

While this example may seem extreme, many people who claim to be Christians will easily turn a blind eye if an injustice puts them in a favourable position. For example, discrimination against a certain people group in a school or college might mean more places for another. Even when it is obvious that such exclusion amounts to injustice, some so-called Christians who benefit from it may choose to ignore the unfairness because of what they derive from it.

One good way to measure our love is to check our reaction towards injustice and truth. If we rejoice about injustice and reject the truth, we are clearly not walking in 'The Most Excellent Way'.

Chapter 13

LOVE NEVER GIVES UP...

Love Never Gives Up

The story of the Prodigal Son ranks amongst the most told stories of the Bible. I can still remember learning this story as a child in Sunday school and I, like many, have read or heard sermons preached about this story so many times.

Amongst other lessons that we can learn from this story that was told to us by our Lord and Saviour Jesus Christ is the truth that love never gives up. One would have imagined that after the injustice done by the son (in this story), the father would have forgotten him and moved on. The story, however, relays to us a great depth of excellent love in practice – the father's longing wait for his son's return despite his sinful actions.

The son had squandered his inheritance and after suffering for a while, he remembered the loving benevolence of his father even towards his servants and decided to return home (not as a son but as a servant):

"When he finally came to his senses, he said to himself, 'At home even the hired servants have food enough to spare, and here I am dying of hunger! I will go home to my father and say, "Father, I have sinned against both heaven and you, and I am no longer worthy of being called your son. Please take me on as a hired servant."'

"So he returned home to his father. And while he was still a long way off, his father saw him coming. Filled with love and compassion, he ran to his son, embraced him, and kissed him. His son said to him, 'Father, I have sinned against both heaven and you, and I am no longer worthy of being called your son.'

"But his father said to the servants, 'Quick! Bring the finest robe in the house and put it on him. Get a ring for his finger and sandals for his feet. And kill the calf we have been fattening. We must celebrate with a feast, for this son of mine was dead and has now returned to life.

He was lost, but now he is found.' So the party began."
Luke 15:17–24

I cannot tell how many times I have heard or read this story before and after I committed my life to Jesus, but I have never ceased to be awed by it – particularly after becoming a Christian and having had the ability to truly understand its meaning.

Whereas Satan treats his loyal servants with great contempt and they can never receive any true and lasting blessing from him, God's love for His servants is immeasurable and transcends beyond what they may or may not have done.

God does not give up on His children and He rejoices greatly when a sinner repents, because it amounts to a gain for His kingdom and a loss for the kingdom of Satan. In His message through the prophet Ezekiel, God declared:

"Do you think that I like to see wicked people die? says the Sovereign LORD. Of course not! I want them to turn from their wicked ways and live." Ezekiel 18:23

Also, in his letter to Timothy, Paul urged that Christians should pray for all men because...

This is good and pleases God our Saviour, who wants everyone to be saved and to understand the truth. 1 Timothy 2:3–4

The extent of love expressed by the father in Jesus' story is excellent and godlike. It is a kind of love that overlooks the wrongdoing done to it and is willing to go an extra mile. It "never loses faith, is always hopeful"…

Love Never Loses Faith, is Always Hopeful

I grew up to know that my late father never gave up on anyone. I often overheard people (particularly members of the family) querying why he continued to assist certain people even after they had let him down.

I remember vaguely how a distant family member he had employed in one of his businesses had been caught stealing from him. As this person had committed other offences, the expectation was that my dad would fire him and wash his hands of him – but he didn't.

What was more surprising to me was that other members of the family were angrier at this person than my dad whom he had stolen from. I saw him build confidence in people who others would have written off, because he was hopeful that with some support they would turn their lives around.

In some translation of the Bible, not losing faith in someone is rendered as 'bearing all things'. While my dad never condoned the wrongdoing done by this person and others who behaved badly toward him, he was willing to forbear, hoping that his forbearance would lead to their repentance. This is an act of deep love that is further demonstrated by a willingness to "cover a multitude of sins".

Most important of all, continue to show deep love for each other, for love covers a multitude of sins. 1 Peter 4:8

Hopeful love does not only see in the present but looks with the eyes of faith into the future. It prefers to see the best in people, and as such treats them in a way that will bring out the goodness that is in them.

I often wonder what would have become of John Mark in the book of Acts if Barnabas hadn't chosen to exercise some level of faith and hope in him. In spite of Mark's shortcoming at the time, Barnabas continued to mentor him (perhaps because they were related since Mark was Barnabas' cousin), and interestingly Mark, in later life, was referred to by Paul the apostle as a co-worker again, even though Paul had previously rejected him. This suggests a reconciliation occurred:

> After some time Paul said to Barnabas, "Let's go back and visit each city where we previously preached the word of the Lord, to see how the new believers are doing." Barnabas agreed and wanted to take along John Mark. But Paul disagreed strongly, since John Mark had deserted them in Pamphylia and had not continued with them in their work. Their disagreement was so sharp that they separated. Barnabas took John Mark with him and sailed for Cyprus. Paul chose Silas, and as he left, the believers entrusted him to the Lord's gracious care. Then he travelled throughout Syria and Cilicia, strengthening the churches there. Acts 15:36–41

> Epaphras, my fellow prisoner in Christ Jesus, sends you his greetings. So do Mark, Aristarchus, Demas, and Luke, my co-workers. Philemon 1:23–24

As we exercise discipline in love, let us also remember never to give up or lose faith but continue to be hopeful.

Chapter 14

LOVE WILL LAST FOREVER

Prophecy and speaking in unknown languages and special knowledge will become useless. But love will last forever! Now our knowledge is partial and incomplete, and even the gift of prophecy reveals only part of the whole picture! But when the time of perfection comes, these partial things will become useless.

When I was a child, I spoke and thought and reasoned as a child. But when I grew up, I put away childish things. Now we see things imperfectly, like puzzling reflections in a mirror, but then we will see everything with perfect clarity. All that I know now is partial and incomplete, but then I will know everything completely, just as God now knows me completely.

Three things will last forever—faith, hope,

and love—and the greatest of these is love.
1 Corinthians 13:8–13

Spiritual gifts are amazing and definitely bring so much flavour into our walk with God, but if they are not combined with godly character and exercised in love they "will become useless" and may even turn out to become the adversary of those who operate in them.

In Matthew's gospel, our Lord Jesus gave us an insight into what will happen in the end to those who operate spiritual gifts without walking in love and godly character. He said:

"Not everyone who calls out to me, 'Lord! Lord!' will enter the Kingdom of Heaven. Only those who actually do the will of my Father in heaven will enter. On judgment day many will say to me, 'Lord! Lord! We prophesied in your name and cast out demons in your name and performed many miracles in your name.' But I will reply, 'I never knew you. Get away from me, you who break God's laws.'"
Matthew 7:21–23

It is important to note that Jesus never denied the fact that these people prophesied in His name, cast out demons in His name and even performed miracles in His name. In spite of the fact that they did all of these "amazing" things, Jesus still rejected them – not because of the "amazing" things they did but because they did not walk in God's righteousness and love.

Interestingly, in another chapter of Matthew's gospel, our Lord Jesus gave us a clear indication of how we must walk through 'The Most Excellent Way' if we want to be welcomed into His kingdom and receive His commendation.

> "But when the Son of Man comes in his glory, and all the angels with him, then he will sit upon his glorious throne. All the nations will be gathered in his presence, and he will separate the people as a shepherd separates the sheep from the goats. He will place the sheep at his right hand and the goats at his left.

> "Then the King will say to those on his right, 'Come, you who are blessed by my Father, inherit the Kingdom prepared for you from the creation of the world. For I was hungry, and you fed me. I was thirsty, and you gave me a drink. I was a stranger, and you invited me into your home. I was naked, and you gave me clothing. I was sick, and you cared for me. I was in prison, and you visited me.'

"Then these righteous ones will reply, 'Lord, when did we ever see you hungry and feed you? Or thirsty and give you something to drink? Or a stranger and show you hospitality? Or naked and give you clothing? When did we ever see you sick or in prison and visit you?'

"And the King will say, 'I tell you the truth, when you did it to one of the least of these my brothers and sisters, you were doing it to me!'

"Then the King will turn to those on the left and say, 'Away with you, you cursed ones, into the eternal fire prepared for the devil and his demons. For I was hungry, and you didn't feed me. I was thirsty, and you didn't give me a drink. I was a stranger, and you didn't invite me into your home. I was naked, and you didn't give me clothing. I was sick and in prison, and you didn't visit me.'

"Then they will reply, 'Lord, when did we ever see you hungry or thirsty or a stranger or naked or sick or in prison, and not help you?'

"And he will answer, 'I tell you the truth, when you refused *to help the least of these my brothers and sisters, you were refusing to help me.'*

"And they will go away into eternal punishment, but the righteous will go into eternal life." Matthew 25:31–46

From reading this passage, it is clear to me that 'The Most Excellent Way' is the way to our Lord's heart; it is the way of kindness, love and sacrifice; it is the way to receive His commendation and reward. Any Christian life that will receive our Lord's commendation must pass through this way, as any other way short of this will only lead to regret and condemnation.

It is my prayer that all who read this book will make a lifelong commitment to walk through 'The Most Excellent Way'.